A Christmas Treasury

This book belongs to

_____

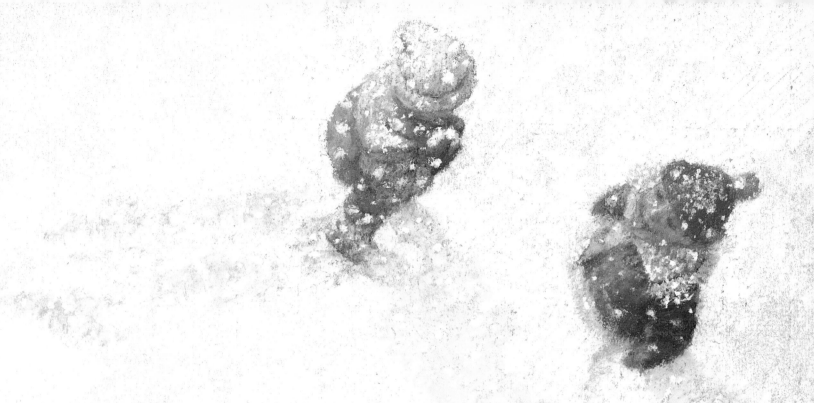

# A CHRISTMAS TREASURY

## The Children's Classic Edition

Illustrated by Christian Birmingham

COURAGE
BOOKS
AN IMPRINT OF RUNNING PRESS
PHILADELPHIA · LONDON

© 1997 by Running Press

Illustrations © 1997 by Christian Birmingham

All rights reserved under the Pan-American and
International Copyright Conventions

Printed in China

9   8   7   6   5   4   3   2   1

Digit on the right indicates the number of this printing

Library of Congress Cataloging-in-Publication Number 96-71141

ISBN 0-7624-0075-7

Designed by Frances J. Soo Ping Chow
Edited by Elaine M. Bucher
Typography: Adobe Caslon and Felix Titling MT

Published by Courage Books, an imprint of
Running Press Book Publishers
125 South Twenty-second Street
Philadelphia, Pennsylvania 19103-4399

# Contents

# The First Christmas
## Luke 2:1–17

And it came to pass in those days, that there went out a decree from Caesar Augustus that all the world should be taxed. . . . And all went to be taxed, every one to his own city. And Joseph also went up from Galilee from the city of Nazareth, into Judaea to the city of David, which is called Bethlehem (because he was of the house and lineage of David), to be taxed with Mary his espoused being great with child. And so it was, that, while they were there the days were accomplished that she delivered. And she brought forth her firstborn and wrapped him in swaddling clothes, and laid him in a manger; because there was no room for them in the inn.

And there were in the same country shepherds abiding in the field, keeping watch over their flock by night. And, lo, the angel of the Lord came upon them, and the glory of the Lord shone round about them, and they were sore afraid. And the angel said unto them, Fear not: for, behold, I bring you good tidings of great joy, which shall be to all people. For unto you is born this day in the city of David a Saviour, which is Christ the Lord. And this *shall* be a sign unto you; Ye shall find the babe wrapped in swaddling clothes, lying in a manger. And suddenly there was with the angel a multitude of the heavenly host praising God, and saying, Glory to God in the highest, and on earth peace, good will toward men.

And it came to pass, as the angels were gone aways from them into heaven, the shepherds said one to another, Let us now go even unto Bethlehem, and see this thing which is come to pass, which the Lord hath made known unto us. And they came with haste, and found Mary, and Joseph, and the babe lying in a manger. And when they had seen *it,* they made known abroad the saying which was told them concerning this child.

# A Merry Christmas

from *Little Women* by Louisa May Alcott

Jo was the first to wake in the gray dawn of Christmas morning. No stockings hung at the fireplace, and for a moment she felt as much disappointed as she did long ago, when her little sock fell down because it was so crammed with goodies. Then she remembered her mother's promise, and slipping her hand under her pillow, drew out a little crimson-covered book. She knew it very well, for it was that beautiful old story of the best life ever lived, and Jo felt that it was a true guide-book for any pilgrim going the long journey. She woke Meg with a "Merry Christmas," and bade her see what was under her pillow. A green-covered book appeared, with the same picture inside, and a few words written by their mother, which made their one present very precious in their eyes. Presently Beth and Amy woke, to rummage and find their little books also,—one dove-colored, the other blue; and all sat looking at and talking about them, while the East grew rosy with the coming day.

In spite of her small vanities, Margaret had a sweet and pious nature, which unconsciously influenced her sisters, especially Jo, who loved her very tenderly, and obeyed her because her advice was so gently given.

"Girls," said Meg, seriously, looking from the tumbled head beside her to the two little night-capped ones in the room beyond, "mother wants us to read and love and mind these books, and we must begin at once. We used to be faithful about it; but since father went away, and all this war trouble unsettled us, we have neglected many things. You can do as you please; but *I* shall keep my book on the table here, and read a little every morning as soon as I wake, for I know it will do me good, and help me through the day."

Then she opened her new book and began to read. Jo put her arm round her, and, leaning cheek to cheek, read also, with the quiet expression so seldom seen on her restless face.

"How good Meg is! Come, Amy, let's do as they do. I'll help you with the hard words, and they'll explain things if we don't understand," whispered Beth, very much impressed by the pretty books and her sister's example.

"I'm glad mine is blue," said Amy; and then the rooms were very still while the pages were softly turned, and the winter sunshine crept in to touch the bright heads and serious faces with a Christmas greeting.

"Where is mother?" asked Meg, as she and Jo ran down to thank her for their gifts, half an hour later.

"Goodness only knows. Some poor creeter come a-beggin', and your ma went straight off to see what was needed. There never *was* such a woman for givin' away vittles and drink, clothes and firin'," replied Hannah, who had lived with the family since Meg was born, and was considered by them all more as a friend than a servant.

"She will be back soon, I guess; so do your cakes, and have everything ready," said Meg, looking over the presents which were collected in a basket and kept under the sofa, ready to be produced at the proper time. "Why, where is Amy's bottle of Cologne?" she added, as the little flask did not appear.

"She took it out a minute ago, and went off with it to put a ribbon on it, or some such notion," replied Jo, dancing about the room to take the first stiffness off the new army-slippers.

"How nice my handkerchiefs look, don't they? Hannah washed and ironed them for me, and I marked them all myself," said Beth, looking proudly at the somewhat uneven letters which had cost her such labor.

"Bless the child, she's gone and put 'Mother' on them instead of 'M. March;' how funny!" cried Jo, taking up one.

"Isn't it right? I thought it was better to do it so, because Meg's initials are 'M. M.,' and I don't want any one to use these but Marmee," said Beth, looking troubled.

"It's all right, dear, and a very pretty idea; quite sensible, too, for no one can ever mistake now. It will please her very much, I know," said Meg, with a frown for Jo, and a smile for Beth.

"There's mother; hide the basket, quick!" cried Jo, as a door slammed, and steps sounded in the hall.

Amy came in hastily, and looked rather abashed when she saw her sisters all waiting for her.

"Where have you been, and what are you hiding behind you?" asked Meg, surprised to see, by her hood and cloak, that lazy Amy had been out so early.

"Don't laugh at me, Jo, I didn't mean any one should know till the time came. I only meant to change the little bottle for a big one, and I gave *all* my money to get it, and I'm truly trying not to be selfish any more."

As she spoke, Amy showed the handsome flask which replaced the cheap one; and looked so earnest and humble in her little effort to forget herself, that Meg hugged her on the spot, and Jo pronounced her "a trump," while Beth ran to the window, and picked her finest rose to ornament the stately bottle.

"You see I felt ashamed of my present, after reading and talking about being good this morning, so I ran round the corner and changed it the minute I was up; and I'm *so* glad, for mine is the handsomest now."

Another bang of the street-door sent the basket under the sofa, and the girls to the table eager for breakfast.

"Merry Christmas, Marmee! Lots of them! Thank you for our books; we read some, and mean to every day," they cried, in chorus.

"Merry Christmas, little daughters! I'm glad you began at once, and hope you will keep on. But I want to say one word before we sit down. Not far away from here lies a poor woman with a little new-born baby. Six children are huddled into one bed to keep from freezing, for they have no fire. There is nothing to eat over there; and the oldest boy came to tell me they were suffering hunger and cold. My girls, will you give them your breakfast as a Christmas present?"

They were all unusually hungry, having waited nearly an hour, and for a minute no one spoke; only a minute, for Jo exclaimed impetuously,—

"I'm so glad you came before we began!"

"May I go and help carry the things to the poor little children?" asked Beth, eagerly.

"*I* shall take the cream and the muffins," added Amy, heroically giving up the articles she most liked.

Meg was already covering the buckwheats, and piling the bread into one big plate.

"I thought you'd do it," said Mrs. March, smiling as if satisfied. "You shall all go and help me, and when we come back we will have bread and milk for breakfast, and make it up at dinner-time."

They were soon ready, and the procession set out. Fortunately it was early, and they went through back streets, so few people saw them, and no one laughed at the funny party.

A poor, bare, miserable room it was, with broken windows, no fire, ragged bed-clothes, a sick mother, wailing baby, and a group of pale, hungry children cuddled under one old quilt, trying to keep warm. How the big eyes stared, and the blue lips smiled, as the girls went in!

"Ach, mein Gott! it is good angels come to us!" cried the poor woman, crying for joy.

"Funny angels in hoods and mittens," said Jo, and set them laughing.

In a few minutes it really did seem as if kind spirits had been at work there. Hannah, who had carried wood, made a fire, and stopped up the broken panes with old hats, and her own shawl. Mrs. March gave the mother tea and gruel, and comforted her with promises of help, while she dressed the little baby as tenderly as if it had been her own. The girls, meantime, spread the table, set the children round the fire, and fed them like so many hungry birds; laughing, talking, and trying to understand the funny broken English.

"Das ist gute!" "Der angel-kinder!" cried the poor things, as they ate, and warmed their purple hands at the comfortable blaze. The girls had never been called angel children before, and thought it very agreeable, especially Jo, who had been considered "a Sancho" ever since she was born. That was a very happy breakfast, though they didn't get any of

it; and when they went away, leaving comfort behind, I think there were not in all the city four merrier people than the hungry little girls who gave away their breakfasts, and contented themselves with bread and milk on Christmas morning.

"That's loving our neighbor better than ourselves, and I like it," said Meg, as they set out their presents, while their mother was up stairs collecting clothes for the poor Hummels.

Not a very splendid show, but there was a great deal of love done up in the few little bundles; and the tall vase of red roses, white chrysanthemums, and trailing vines, which stood in the middle, gave quite an elegant air to the table.

"She's coming! strike up, Beth, open the door, Amy. Three cheers for Marmee! cried Jo, prancing about, while Meg went to conduct mother to the seat of honor.

Beth played her gayest march, Amy threw open the door, and Meg enacted escort with great dignity. Mrs. March was both surprised and touched; and smiled with her eyes full as she examined her presents, and read the little notes which accompanied them. The slippers went on at once, a new handkerchief was slipped into her pocket, well scented with Amy's Cologne, the rose was fastened in her bosom, and the nice gloves were pronounced "a perfect fit."

There was a good deal of laughing, and kissing, and explaining, in the simple, loving fashion which makes these home-festivals so pleasant at the time, so sweet to remember long afterward.

# Christmas Every Day
## William Dean Howells

Well, once there was a little girl who liked Christmas so much that she wanted it to be Christmas every day in the year; and as soon as Thanksgiving was over she began to send postal cards to the old Christmas Fairy to ask if she mightn't have it. In about three weeks—or just the day before Christmas, it was—she got a letter from the Fairy, saying she might have it Christmas every day for a year, and then they would see about having it longer.

The little girl was a good deal excited already, preparing for the old-fashioned, once-a-year Christmas that was coming the next day, and perhaps the Fairy's promise didn't make such an impression on her as it would have made at some other time. She just resolved to keep it to herself, and surprise everybody with it as it kept coming true: and then it slipped out of her mind altogether.

She had a splendid Christmas. She went to bed early, so as to let Santa Claus have a chance at the stockings, and in the morning she was up the first of anybody and went and felt them, and found hers all lumpy with packages of candy, and oranges and grapes, and pocketbooks and rubber balls and all kinds of small presents just as they always had every Christmas. Then she waited around till the rest of the family were up, and she was the first to burst into the library, when the doors were opened, and look at the large presents laid out on the library table—books, and dolls, and little stoves, and dozens of handkerchiefs, and ink stands, and skates, and snow shovels, and photograph frames, and little easels, and boxes of watercolors, and candied cherries, and doll's houses, and the big Christmas tree, lighted and standing in the middle.

She had a splendid Christmas all day. She ate so much candy that she did not want any breakfast; and the whole forenoon the presents kept pouring in and she went 'round giving the presents she had got for other people, and came home and ate turkey and cranberry for dinner, and plum-pudding and nuts and raisins and oranges and more candy, and then

went and coasted and came in with a stomachache, crying; and they had a light supper, and pretty early everybody went to bed cross.

The little girl slept very heavily, and she slept very late, but she was wakened at last by the other children dancing 'round her bed with their stockings full of presents in their hands.

"What is it?" said the little girl, and she rubbed her eyes and tried to rise up in bed.

"Christmas! Christmas! Christmas!" they all shouted, and waved their stockings.

"Nonsense! It was Christmas yesterday."

Her brothers and sisters just laughed. "We don't know about that. It's Christmas today, any way. You come into the library and see."

Then all at once it flashed on the little girl that the Fairy was keeping her promise, and her year of Christmases was beginning. She was dreadfully sleepy, but she sprang up like a lark—a lark that had overeaten itself and gone to bed cross—and darted into the library. There it was again! The Christmas tree blazing away, and the family picking out their presents, but looking pretty sleepy, and her father perfectly puzzled, and her mother ready to cry.

"I'm sure I don't see how I'm to dispose of all these things," said her mother, and her father said it seemed to him they had had something just like it the day before, but he must have dreamed it. Well, the next day, it was just the same thing over again, but everybody getting crosser; and at the end of a week's time so many people had lost their tempers that they perfectly strewed the ground. Even when people tried to recover their tempers they usually got somebody else's, and it made the most dreadful mix.

The little girl began to get frightened, keeping the secret all to herself; she wanted to tell her mother, but she didn't dare to; and she was ashamed to ask the Fairy to take back her gift, it seemed ungrateful, and she thought she would try to stand it, but she hardly knew how she could, for a whole year. So it went on and on, and it was Christmas on St. Valentine's Day, and Washington's Birthday just

the same as any day, and it didn't skip even the First of April, though everything was counterfeit that day, and that was some *little* relief.

After a while, turkeys got to be so scarce that they were about a thousand dollars apiece, and they got to passing off almost anything for turkey. And the cranberries—well, they asked a diamond apiece for cranberries. All the woods and orchards were cut down for Christmas trees and where the woods and orchards used to be, it looked just like a stubblefield, with the stumps. After a while they had to make Christmas trees out of rags, and stuff them with bran, like old-fashioned dolls; but there were plenty of rags, because people got so poor, buying presents for one another, that they couldn't get any new clothes, and they just wore their old ones to tatters. It was perfectly shameful.

Well, after it had gone on about three or four months, the little girl, whenever she came into the room in the morning and saw those great ugly lumpy stockings dangling at the fireplace, and the disgusting presents around everywhere, used to just sit down and burst out crying. In six months she was perfectly exhausted; she couldn't even cry any more, she just slammed her presents across the room.

By that time people didn't carry presents around nicely any more. They flung them over the fence, or through the window, or anything; and, instead of taking great pains to write "For dear Papa," or "Mamma," or "Brother," or "Sister," or "Susie," or "Sammie," or "Billie," or whoever it was, and troubling to get the spelling right, and then signing their names, and "Xmas, 188_," they used to write in the gift books, "Take it, you horrid old thing!" and then go and bang it against the front door. Nearly everybody had built barns to hold their presents, but pretty soon the barns overflowed, and then they used to let them lie out in the rain, or anywhere. Sometimes the police used to come and tell them to shovel their presents off the sidewalk, or they would arrest them.

Well, before it came Thanksgiving, it had leaked out who had caused all these Christmases. The little girl had suffered so much that she had talked about it in her sleep; and after that, hardly anybody would play with her. People just perfectly despised her, because if it had not been for her greediness, it wouldn't have happened; and now, when it came Thanksgiving, and she wanted them to go to church, and have squash-pie and turkey, and show their gratitude, they said that all the turkeys had been eaten up for her old Christmas dinners, and if she would stop the Christmases, they would see about the gratitude. And the very next day the little girl began to send letters to the Christmas Fairy, and then telegrams, to stop it. But it didn't do any good; and then she got to calling at the Fairy's house, but the girl that came to the door always said "Not at home," or "Engaged," or "At dinner," or something like that; and so it went on till it came to the old once-a-year Christmas Eve. The little girl fell asleep, and when she woke up in the morning—it wasn't Christmas at last.

Well, there was the greatest rejoicing all over the country, and it extended clear up into Canada. The people met together everywhere, and kissed and cried for joy. The city carts went around and gathered up all the candy and raisins and nuts, and dumped them into the river; and it made the fish perfectly sick; and the whole United States, as far out as Alaska, was one blaze of bonfires, where the children were burning their gift-books and presents of all kinds. They had the greatest time!

The little girl went to thank the old Fairy because she had stopped its being Christmas, and she said she hoped she would keep her promise, and see that Christmas never, never came again. Then the Fairy frowned, and asked her if she was sure she knew what she meant; and the little girl asked her, why not? and the old Fairy said that now she was behaving just as greedily as ever, and she'd better look out. This made the little girl think it all over carefully again, and she said she would be willing to have it Christmas about once in a thousand years; and then she said a hundred, and then she said ten, and at last she got down to one. Then the Fairy said that was the good old way that had pleased people ever since Christmas began, and she was agreed. Then the little girl said, "What're your shoes made of?" And the Fairy said, "Leather." And the little girl said, "Bargain's done forever," and skipped off, and hippity-hopped the whole way home.

# Jingle, Bells

Dashing through the snow
　　In a one-horse open sleigh,
O'er the fields we go,
　　Laughing all the way.
Bells on bobtail ring,
　　Making spirits bright.
What fun it is to laugh and sing
　　A sleighing song tonight!

CHORUS:
Jingle, bells! Jingle, bells!
　　Jingle all the way!
Oh, what fun it is to ride
　　In a one-horse open sleigh—hey!
Jingle, bells! Jingle, bells!
　　Jingle all the way!
Oh, what fun it is to ride
　　In a one-horse open sleigh!

A day or two ago,
　　I thought I'd take a ride,
And soon Miss Fannie Bright
　　Was seated by my side.
The horse was lean and lank,
　　But hardly worth his hay.
He veered into a drifted bank
　　And overturned the sleigh!

CHORUS

Now the ground is white.
 Go for it while you're young.
Take the girls tonight
 And sing this sleighing song.
Just rent a bobtail'd bay,
 Two-forty for his speed.
Then hitch him to an open sleigh,
 And crack! you'll take the lead!

CHORUS

You won't mind the cold,
 The robe is thick and warm.
Snow falls on the road,
 Silv'ring every form,
The woods are dark and still.
 The horse is trotting fast.
He'll pull the sleigh around the hill
 And home again at last.

CHORUS

# Deck the Halls

Deck the halls with boughs of holly.
    Fa la la la la, la la la la.
'Tis the season to be jolly.
    Fa la la la la, la la la la.
Don we now our gay apparel.
    Fa la la, la la la, la la la.
Troll the ancient Yuletide carol:
    Fa la la la la, la la la la.

See the blazing Yule before us.
    Fa la la la la, la la la la.
Strike the harp and join the chorus.
    Fa la la la la, la la la la.
Follow me in merry measure—
    Fa la la, la la la, la la la—
While I tell of Yuletide treasure.
    Fa la la la la, la la la la.

Fast away the old year passes.
    Fa la la la la, la la la la.
Hail the new, ye lads and lasses.
    Fa la la la la, la la la la.
Sing we joyous all together—
    Fa la la, la la la, la la la—
Heedless of the wind and weather.
    Fa la la la la, la la la la.

# The First Noel

The first Noel
   the angels did say
Was to certain poor shepherds
   in fields as they lay—
In fields where they lay,
   keeping their sheep,
On a cold winter's night
   that was so deep.

CHORUS:
Noel, Noel, Noel, Noel,
Born is the King of Israel!

They looked up
   and saw a star,
Shining in the East,
   but beyond them far.
And unto the Earth
   it gave great light,
And so it continued,
   both day and night.

CHORUS

And by the light
   of that same star
Three Wise Men came
   from country afar.
To seek for a King
   was their intent,
And to follow the star
   wherever it went.

CHORUS

This star drew nigh
   to the northwest.
Over Bethlehem
   it took its rest,

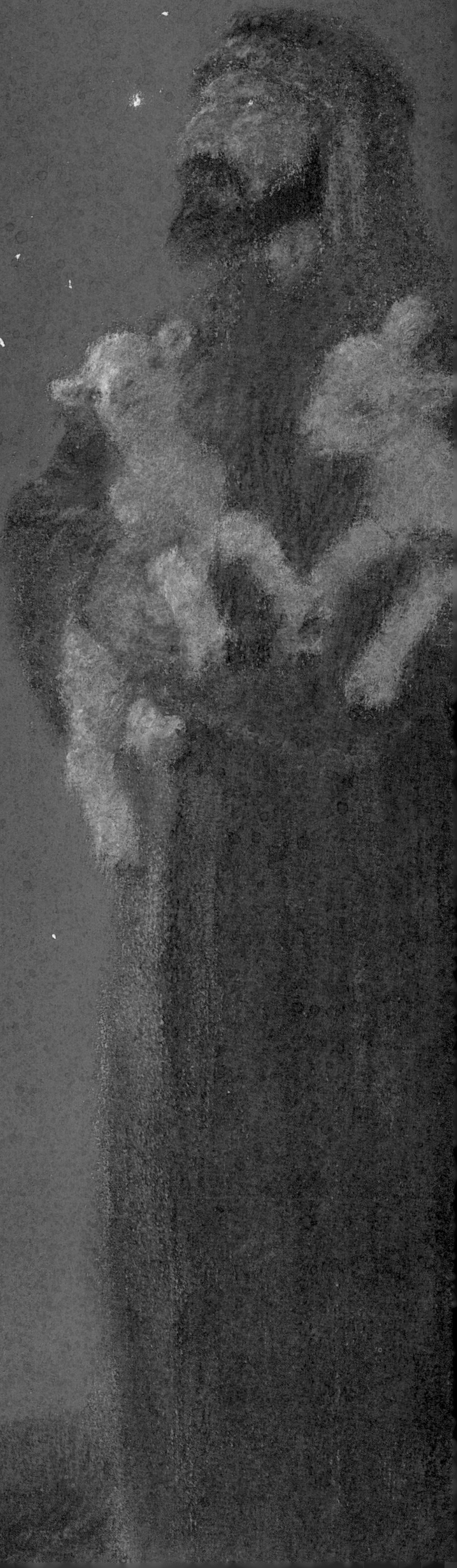

And there it did
    both stop and stay
Right over the stable
    where Jesus lay.

CHORUS

Then they did know
    and in wonder confide
That within that house
    a King did reside.
One entered in then,
    with his own eyes to see
And discovered the Babe
    in poverty.

CHORUS

Between the stalls
    of the oxen, forlorn,
This Child on that cold night
    in truth was born.
And for want of a crib,
    Mary did Him lay
In the depths of a manger
    amongst the hay.

CHORUS

Then entered in
    all those Wise Men three,
Fell reverently
    upon bended knee,
And offered there,
    in His presence,
Gifts of gold and of myrrh
    and of frankincense.

CHORUS

# Silent Night

Silent night, holy night!
  All is calm, all is bright
'Round yon Virgin Mother and Child—
  Holy infant, so tender and mild.
Sleep in heavenly peace,
Sleep in heavenly peace.

Silent night, holy night!
  Shepherds quake at the sight.
Glories stream from Heaven afar,
  Heav'nly hosts sing "Alleluia,
Christ the Savior is born,
Christ the Savior is born!"

Silent night, holy night!
  Son of God, love's pure light,
Radiance beams from Thy holy face,
  With the dawn of redeeming grace.
Jesus, Lord at Thy birth,
Jesus, Lord at Thy birth!

# Away in a Manger

Away in a manger,
    no crib for a bed,
The little Lord Jesus
    laid down His sweet head.
The stars in the heavens
    looked down where He lay:
The little Lord Jesus,
    asleep in the hay.

The cattle are lowing.
    The baby awakes,
But little Lord Jesus,
    no crying he makes.
I love Thee, Lord Jesus!
    Look down from the sky,
And stay by my cradle
    till morning is nigh.

# We Three Kings of Orient Are

We three kings of Orient are.
    Bearing gifts, we traverse afar—
Field and fountain, moor and mountain—
    Following yonder star.

**CHORUS:**
**Oh, star of wonder, star of night,**
**Star of royal beauty bright,**
**Westward leading, still proceeding,**
**Guide us to thy perfect light.**

Born a king on Bethlehem's plain—
    Gold I bring, to crown Him again—
King for ever, ceasing never,
    Over us all to reign.

**CHORUS**

Frankincense to offer have I.
    Incense owns a Deity nigh.
Prayer and praising, all men raising,
    Worship Him, God most high!

**CHORUS**

Myrrh is mine: its bitter perfume
    Breathes a life of gathering gloom,
Sorrowing, sighing, bleeding, dying,
    Sealed in the stone-cold tomb.

**CHORUS**

Glorious now, behold Him arise:
    King and God and sacrifice!
Heav'n sings, "Hallelujah!"
    "Hallelujah!" the Earth replies.

**CHORUS**

# The Twelve Days
# of Christmas

On the first day of Christmas,
My true love gave to me
A partridge in a pear tree.

On the second day of Christmas,
My true love gave to me
Two turtle doves,
and a partridge in a pear tree.

On the third day of Christmas,
My true love gave to me
Three French hens,
Two turtle doves,
and a partridge in a pear tree.

On the fourth day of Christmas,
My true love gave to me
Four calling birds,
Three French hens,
Two turtle doves,
and a partridge in a pear tree.

On the fifth day of Christmas,
My true love gave to me
Five golden rings,
Four calling birds,
Three French hens,
Two turtle doves,
and a partridge in a pear tree.

On the sixth day of Christmas,
My true love gave to me
Six geese a-laying,
Five golden rings,
Four calling birds,
Three French hens,
Two turtle doves,
and a partridge in a pear tree.

On the seventh day of Christmas,
My true love gave to me
Seven swans a-swimming,
Six geese a-laying,
Five golden rings,
Four calling birds,
Three French hens,
Two turtle doves,
and a partridge in a pear tree.

On the eighth day of Christmas,
My true love gave to me
Eight maids a-milking,
Seven swans a-swimming,
Six geese a-laying,
Five golden rings,
Four calling birds,
Three French hens,
Two turtle doves,
and a partridge in a pear tree.

On the ninth day of Christmas,
    My true love gave to me
Nine ladies dancing,
Eight maids a-milking,
Seven swans a-swimming,
Six geese a-laying,
Five golden rings,
Four calling birds,
Three French hens,
Two turtle doves,
    and a partridge in a pear tree.

On the tenth day of Christmas,
    My true love gave to me
Ten lords a-leaping,
Nine ladies dancing,
Eight maids a-milking,
Seven swans a-swimming,
Six geese a-laying,
Five golden rings,
Four calling birds,
Three French hens,
Two turtle doves,
    and a partridge in a pear tree.

On the eleventh day of Christmas,
    My true love gave to me
Eleven pipers piping,
Ten lords a-leaping,

Nine ladies dancing,
Eight maids a-milking,
Seven swans a-swimming,
Six geese a-laying,
Five golden rings,
Four calling birds,
Three French hens,
Two turtle doves,
    and a partridge in a pear tree.

On the twelfth day of Christmas,
    My true love gave to me
Twelve drummers drumming,
Eleven pipers piping,
Ten lords a-leaping,
Nine ladies dancing,
Eight maids a-milking,
Seven swans a-swimming,
Six geese a-laying,
Five golden rings,
Four calling birds,
Three French hens,
Two turtle doves,
    and a partridge in a pear tree.

# We Wish You a Merry Christmas

We wish you a Merry Christmas
 We wish you a Merry Christmas,
We wish you a Merry Christmas,
 And a Happy New Year!

**CHORUS:**
**Glad tidings we bring**
**To you and your kin.**
**We wish you a Merry Christmas**
**And a Happy New Year.**

Oh, bring us some figgy pudding,
 Oh, bring us some figgy pudding,
Oh, bring us some figgy pudding
 And a glass of good cheer!

**CHORUS**

We won't go until we get some,
 We won't go until we get some,
We won't go until we get some
 So bring it right here!

**CHORUS**

We'll sing you some happy carols,
 We'll sing you some happy carols,
We'll sing you some happy carols,
 To ravish your ear!

**CHORUS**

We have quite the finest voices,
 We have quite the finest voices,
We have quite the finest voices
 That you'll ever hear!

**CHORUS**

We wish you a Merry Christmas
 We wish you a Merry Christmas,
We wish you a Merry Christmas,
 And a Happy New Year!

# The Little Blue Dishes

Once upon a time, there was a poor woodcutter who lived with his wife and three children in a log cabin on the edge of town. The eldest boy in the family was named Nicholas, the middle brother was named Robert, and the youngest little sister, who was just five years old, was named Ilsa.

Soon it would be Christmas, so the children went into town to the toymaker's store to look at all the toys. There were dolls nestled in their doll-houses, spinning, colorful tops, toy soldiers lined in a row, and many other wonderful things.

"Ilsa," said Robert, "which toy is your favorite?"

"Oh, that little box of blue dishes," said Ilsa, "that is my favorite of them all!" She imagined how much fun it would be to have tea parties with these dishes, but she knew they were too much money for her family to buy them for her.

On Christmas Eve, the children hung up their stockings, even though they knew they were too poor to expect much this year. After supper, Nicholas went out to play with the other older children. Ilsa and Robert sat by the fire talking about the toys they had seen in town.

"I do so wish I had those little blue dishes," said Ilsa. Soon she became very sleepy and her father carried her off to bed.

As soon as Ilsa drifted off to sleep, Robert ran to his bank. He found only one penny inside, but still ran all the way to the toy store in town to buy his sister a gift.

"What can I buy for one penny?" he asked the toymaker.

"Only a little candy heart with a picture on it." replied the toymaker.

"But I want that set of blue dishes for my sister," said Robert.

"Those cost ten cents," said the man.

"Well, then I'll take the candy heart" said Robert. He hurried home with his package, put it in Ilsa's stocking, and went to bed.

Later that night, Nicholas came home. He was cold and hungry. As he sat by the fire, he noticed how bumpy the bottom of Ilsa's stocking looked.

He reached inside the stocking, and pulled out the candy heart. Before he realized what he was doing, he ate the entire heart. "Oh my," he thought, "that was a gift for Ilsa. I must go and get her another present."

He ran to his bank and removed his savings of ten pennies. He raced to the toy store and found the toymaker ready to close his shop. "What can I buy for ten cents?" Nicholas asked.

"Well, I have very little left," said the man, "but there is still a little set of blue dishes for ten cents."

"I'll take them," said Nicholas. He hurried home and put the dishes in Ilsa's stocking.

Early Christmas morning, the children raced down the stairs to look in their stockings.

"Oh," cried Ilsa, "Look at my stocking!" She was so excited to see the blue dishes tucked inside her stocking.

Robert was amazed. He never understood how his little candy heart magically changed into the box of blue dishes.

# Why the Chimes Rang

## Raymond MacDonald Alden

There was once, in a faraway country where few people have ever traveled, a wonderful church. It stood on a high hill in the midst of a great city; and every Sunday, as well as on sacred days like Christmas, thousands of people climbed the hill to its great archways, looking like lines of ants all moving in the same direction.

When you came to the building itself, you found stone columns and dark passages, and a grand entrance leading to a main room of the church. This room was so long that one standing at the doorway could scarcely see to the other end, where the choir stood by the marble altar. In the farthest corner was the organ; and this organ was so loud that, sometimes when it played, the people for miles around would close their shutters and prepare for a great thunderstorm. Altogether, no such church as this was ever seen before, especially when it was lighted up for some festival, and crowded with people, young and old. But the strangest thing about the whole building was the wonderful chime of bells.

At one corner of the church was a great gray tower, with ivy growing over it as far up as one could see. I say as far as one could see, because the tower was quite great enough to fit the great church, and it rose so far into the sky that it was only in very fair weather that anyone claimed to be able to see the top.

Even then one could not be certain that it was in sight. Up, and up, and up climbed the stones and the ivy; and, as the men who built the church had been dead for hundreds of years, everyone had forgotten how high the tower was supposed to be.

Now all the people knew that at the top of the tower was a chime of Christmas bells. They had hung there ever since the church had been built, and were the most beautiful bells in the world. Some thought it was because a great musician had cast them and arranged them in their place; others said it was because of the great height, which reached up where the air was clearest and purest; however that

might be, no one who had ever heard the chimes denied that they were the sweetest in the world. Some described them as sounding like angels far up in the sky; others, as sounding like strange winds singing throughout the trees.

But the fact was that no one had heard them for years and years. There was an old man living not far from the church, who said that his mother had spoken of hearing them when she was a little girl, and he was the only one who was sure of as much as that. They were Christmas chimes, you see, and were not meant to be played by men or on common days. It was the custom on Christmas Eve for all the people to bring to the church their offerings to the Christ child; and when the greatest and best offering was laid on the altar, there used to come sounding through the music of the choir the Christmas chimes far up in the tower. Some said that the wind rang them, and others that they were so high that the angels could set them swinging. But for many long years they had never been heard. It was said that people had been growing less careful of their gifts for the Christ child, and that no offering was brought, great enough to deserve the music of the chimes.

Every Christmas Eve the rich people still crowded to the altar, each one trying to bring some better gift than any other, without giving anything that he wanted for himself, and the church was crowded with those who thought that perhaps the wonderful bells might be heard again. But although the service was splendid, and the offerings plenty, only the roar of the wind could be heard, far up in the stone tower.

Now, a number of miles from the city, in a little country village, where nothing could be seen of the great church but glimpses of the tower when the weather was fine, lived a boy name Pedro, and his little brother. They knew very little about the Christmas chimes, but they had heard of the service in the church on Christmas Eve, and had a secret

plan, which they had often talked over when by themselves, to go to see the beautiful celebration.

"Nobody can guess, Little Brother," Pedro would say, "all the fine things there are to see and hear; and I have even heard it said that the Christ child sometimes comes down to bless the service. What if we could see Him?"

The day before Christmas was bitterly cold, with a few lonely snowflakes flying in the air, and a hard white crust on the ground. Sure enough, Pedro and Little Brother were able to slip quietly away early in the afternoon; and although the walking was hard in the frosty air, before nightfall they had trudged so far, hand in hand, that they saw the lights of the big city just ahead of them. Indeed, they were about to enter one of the great gates in the wall that surrounded it, when they saw something dark on the snow near their path, and stepped aside to look at it.

It was a poor woman, who had fallen just outside the city, too sick and tired to get in where she might have found shelter. The soft snow made of a drift a sort of pillow for her, and she would soon be so sound asleep, in the wintry air, that no one could ever waken her again.

All this Pedro saw in a moment, and he knelt down beside her and tried to rouse her, even tugging at her arm a little, as though he would have tried to carry her away. He turned her face toward him, so that he could rub some of the snow on it, and when he had looked at her silently a moment he stood up again, and said:

"It's no use, Little Brother. You will have to go on alone."

"Alone?" cried Little Brother. "And you not see the Christmas festival?"

"No," said Pedro, and he could not keep back a bit of a choking sound in his throat. "See this poor woman. Her face looks like the Madonna in the chapel window, and she will freeze to death if nobody cares for her. Everyone has gone to the church now, but when you come back you can bring someone to help her. I will rub her to keep her from freezing, and perhaps get her to eat the bun that is left in my pocket."

"But I cannot bear to leave you, and go on alone," said Little Brother.

"Both of us need not miss the service," said Pedro, "and it had better be I than you. You can easily find your way to the church; and you must see and hear everything twice, Little Brother—once for you and once for me. I am sure the Christ child must know how I should love to come with you and worship Him; and oh! if you get a chance, Little Brother, to slip up to the altar without getting in anyone's way, take this little silver piece of mine, and lay it down for my offering, when no one is looking. Do not forget where you have left me, and forgive me for not going with you."

In this way he hurried Little Brother off to the city, and winked hard to keep back the tears, as he heard the crunching footsteps sounding farther and farther away in the twilight. It was pretty hard to lose the music and splendor of the Christmas celebration that he had been planning for so long, and spend the time instead in that lonely place in the snow.

The great church was a wonderful place that night. Everyone said that it had never looked so bright and beautiful before. When the organ played and the thousands of people sang, the walls shook with the sound, and little Pedro, away outside the city wall, felt the earth tremble around him.

At the close of the service came the procession with the offerings to be laid on the altar. Rich men and great men marched proudly up to lay down their gifts to the Christ child. Some brought wonderful jewels, some baskets of gold so heavy that they could scarcely carry them down the aisle. A great writer laid down a book that he had been making for years and years. And last of all walked the king of the country, hoping with all the rest to win for himself the chime of the Christmas bells. There went a great murmur throughout the church, as the people saw the king take from his head the royal crown, all set with precious stones, and lay it gleaming on the altar, as his offering to the Holy Child. "Surely," everyone said, "we shall hear the bells now, for nothing like this has ever happened before."

But still only the cold old wind was heard in the tower, and the people shook their heads; and some of them said, as they had before, that they never really believed the story of the chimes, and doubted if they ever rang at all.

The procession was over, and the choir began the closing hymn. Suddenly the organist stopped playing as though he had been shot, and everyone looked at the old minister, who was standing by the altar, holding up his hand for silence. Not a sound could be heard from anyone in the church, but as all the people strained their ears to listen, there came softly, but distinctly, swinging through the air, the sound of the chimes in the tower. So far away, and yet so clear the music seemed—so much sweeter were the notes than anything that had been heard before, rising and falling away up there in the sky, that the people in the church sat for a moment as still as though something held each of them by the shoulders. Then they all stood up together and stared straight at the altar, to see what great gift had awakened the long-silent bells.

But all that the nearest of them saw was the childish figure of Little Brother, who had crept softly down the aisle when no one was looking, and had laid Pedro's little piece of silver on the altar.

# The Night Before Christmas
## Clement C. Moore

'Twas the night before Christmas,
   when all through the house
Not a creature was stirring,
   not even a mouse;
The stockings were hung
   by the chimney with care,
In hopes that St. Nicholas
   soon would be there;
The children were nestled
   all snug in their beds,
While visions of sugar-plums
   danced through their heads;
And mamma in her kerchief,
   and I in my cap,
Had just settled our brains
   for a long winter's nap,—
When out on the lawn
   there arose such a clatter,
I sprang from my bed
   to see what was the matter.
Away to the window
   I flew like a flash,
Tore open the shutters
   and threw up the sash.
The moon, on the breast
   of the new-fallen snow,

Gave a lustre of midday
   to objects below;
When what to my wondering eyes
   should appear,
But a miniature sleigh
   and eight tiny reindeer,
With a little old driver,
   so lively and quick
I knew in a moment
   it must be St. Nick.
More rapid than eagles
   his coursers they came,
And he whistled and shouted
   and called them by name;
"Now, Dasher! now, Dancer!
   now, Prancer and Vixen!
On, Comet! on, Cupid!
   on, Donder and Blitzen!
To the top of the porch,
   to the top of the wall!
Now, dash away, dash away,
   dash away all!"
As dry leaves that before
   the wild hurricane fly,
When they meet with an obstacle,
   mount to the sky,

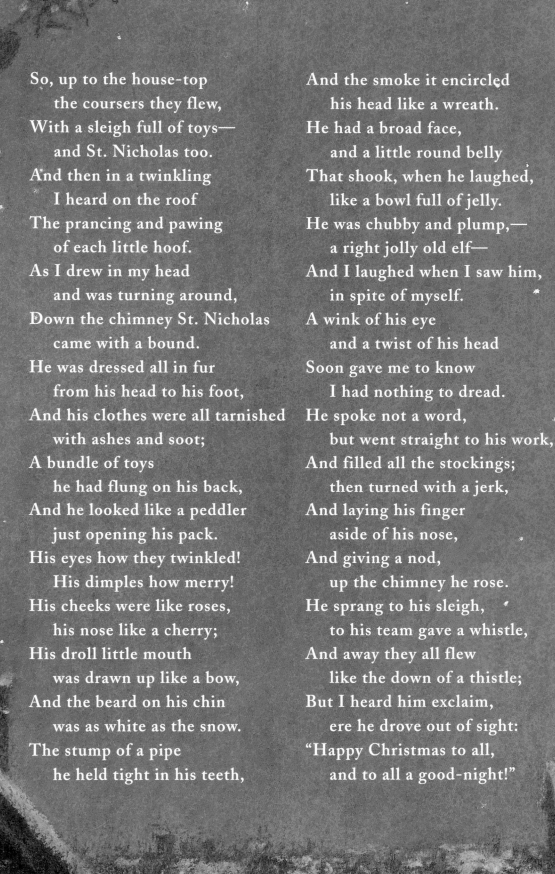

So, up to the house-top
   the coursers they flew,
With a sleigh full of toys—
   and St. Nicholas too.
And then in a twinkling
   I heard on the roof
The prancing and pawing
   of each little hoof.
As I drew in my head
   and was turning around,
Down the chimney St. Nicholas
   came with a bound.
He was dressed all in fur
   from his head to his foot,
And his clothes were all tarnished
   with ashes and soot;
A bundle of toys
   he had flung on his back,
And he looked like a peddler
   just opening his pack.
His eyes how they twinkled!
   His dimples how merry!
His cheeks were like roses,
   his nose like a cherry;
His droll little mouth
   was drawn up like a bow,
And the beard on his chin
   was as white as the snow.
The stump of a pipe
   he held tight in his teeth,

And the smoke it encircled
   his head like a wreath.
He had a broad face,
   and a little round belly
That shook, when he laughed,
   like a bowl full of jelly.
He was chubby and plump,—
   a right jolly old elf—
And I laughed when I saw him,
   in spite of myself.
A wink of his eye
   and a twist of his head
Soon gave me to know
   I had nothing to dread.
He spoke not a word,
   but went straight to his work,
And filled all the stockings;
   then turned with a jerk,
And laying his finger
   aside of his nose,
And giving a nod,
   up the chimney he rose.
He sprang to his sleigh,
   to his team gave a whistle,
And away they all flew
   like the down of a thistle;
But I heard him exclaim,
   ere he drove out of sight:
"Happy Christmas to all,
   and to all a good-night!"

# Merry Christmas

**M** for the **M**usic, merry and clear;
**E** for the **E**ve, the crown of the year;
**R** for the **R**omping of bright girls and boys;
**R** for the **R**eindeer that bring them the toys;
**Y** for the **Y**ule-log softly aglow.

**C** for the **C**old of the sky and the snow;
**H** for the **H**earth where they hang up the hose;
**R** for the **R**eel which the old folks propose;
**I** for the **I**cicles seen through the pane;
**S** for the **S**leigh bells, with tinkling refrain;
**T** for the **T**ree with gifts all abloom;
**M** for the **M**istletoe hung in the room;
**A** for the **A**nthems we all love to hear;
**S** for **St. Nicholas**—joy of the year!

**from *St. Nicholas* magazine**

# The Friendly Beasts

Jesus, our brother, kind and good
Was humbly born in a stable rude.
And the friendly beasts around him stood,
Jesus, our brother, kind and good.

"I," said the donkey, shaggy and brown,
"I carried His mother uphill and down,
I carried her safely to Bethlehem town."
"I," said the donkey, shaggy and brown.

"I," said the cow, all white and red,
"I gave Him my manger for His bed,
I gave Him my hay to pillow His head."
"I," said the cow, all white and red.

"I," said the sheep with the curly horn,
"I gave Him my wool, for His blanket warm
He wore my coat on Christmas morn."
"I," said the sheep with the curly horn.

"I," said the dove from the rafters high,
"Cooed Him to sleep, that He should not cry,
We cooed Him to sleep, my mate and I."
"I," said the dove from the rafters high.

So every beast by some good spell,
In the stable dark was glad to tell
Of the gift he gave Emmanuel.
The gift he gave Emmanuel.

**an old English Christmas carol**

# Christmas Song

Why do bells for Christmas ring?
Why do little children sing?

Once a lovely shining star,
Seen by shepherds from afar,
Gently moved until its light
Made a manger's cradle bright.

There a darling baby lay,
Pillowed soft upon the hay;
And its mother sang and smiled,
"This is Christ, the holy Child!"

Therefore bells for Christmas ring,
Therefore little children sing.

Eugene Field

# Yes, Virginia,
# There Is a Santa Claus

In 1897, a young girl wrote to the *New York Sun* asking whether Santa Claus truly existed. The paper's response, written by Francis P. Church, appeared in *The Sun* on Sept. 21, 1897. *Is There a Santa Claus?* We take pleasure in answering at once and thus prominently the communication below, expressing at the same time our great gratification that its faithful author is numbered among the friends of *The Sun:*

"Dear Editor: I am eight years old. Some of my little friends say there is no Santa Claus. Papa says 'if you see it in *The Sun* it's so.' Please tell me the truth; is there a Santa Claus?"

Virginia O'Hanlon.

Virginia, your little friends are wrong. They have been affected by the skepticism of a skeptical age. They do not believe except they see. They think that nothing can be which is not comprehensible by their little minds. All minds, Virginia, whether they be men's or children's, are little. In this great universe of ours man is a mere insect, an ant, in his intellect, as compared with the boundless world about him, as measured by the intelligence capable of grasping the whole of truth and knowledge.

Yes, Virginia, there is a Santa Claus. He exists as certainly as love and generosity and devotion exist, and you know that they abound and give to our life its highest beauty and joy. Alas! how dreary would be the world if there were no Santa Claus. It would be as dreary as if there were no Virginias. There would be no childlike faith then, no poetry, no romance, to make tolerable this existence. We should have no enjoyment, except in sense and sight. The eternal light with which childhood fills the world would be extinguished.

Not believe in Santa Claus! You might as well not believe in fairies! You might get your papa to hire men to watch in all the chimneys on Christmas eve to catch Santa Claus, but even if they did not see Santa Claus coming down, what would that prove? Nobody sees Santa Claus, but that is no sign that there is no Santa Claus. The most real things in the world are those that neither children nor men can see. Did you ever see fairies dancing on the lawn? Of course not, but that's no proof that they are not there. Nobody can conceive or imagine all the wonders there are unseen and unseeable in the world.

You may tear apart the baby's rattle and see what makes the noise inside, but there is a veil covering the unseen world which not the strongest man, nor even the united strength of all the strongest men that ever lived, could tear apart. Only faith, fancy, poetry, love, romance, can push aside that curtain and view and picture the supernal beauty and glory beyond. Is it all real? Ah, Virginia, in all this world there is nothing else real and abiding.

No Santa Claus! Thank God he lives, and he lives forever. A thousand years from now, Virginia, nay, ten times ten thousand years from now, he will continue to make glad the heart of childhood.